You Know Your Dog Owns You If...

A baRKfoRd Book

By Chaz Chapman and Stacy Curtis

BOWTIE
P R E S S

Irvine, California

Karla Austin, Business Operations Manager
Jen Dorsey, Associate Editor
Michelle Martinez, Editor
Rebekah Bryant, Editorial Assistant
Erin Kuechenmeister, Production Editor
Ruth Strother, Editor-at-Large
Nick Clemente, Special Consultant
Michael Vincent Capozzi, cover design
Vicky Vaughn, interior design and layout

Library of Congress Control Number: 2003114025
ISBN 1-931993-39-4

BowTie Press®
A Division of BowTie, Inc.
3 Burroughs
Irvine, CA 92618

Printed and Bound in Singapore
10 9 8 7 6 5 4 3 2

Dedication

To the creator of my world, my wife, and my daughter—the three most important beings in my life. And to my dog, Zoë, my muse for Barkford.
—Chaz

.

To Mom and Dad. Thanks for all the pencils and paper.
—Stacy

Foreword

As I type this, my dog, Zoë, is sleeping by my feet. Just now, she looked at me with an annoyed expression on her face, and got up and left the room. Apparently I was typing too loudly. Tomorrow I'll go shopping for a quieter keyboard, but for now I need to finish this foreword.

I always dreamed of having a dog who would bring me my newspaper in the morning and fetch my slippers in the evening. But I didn't get that kind of dog; my dog, Zoë, is more like a princess. Zoë came into our home a few years ago, and I quickly got caught up in her life. I began spending more time and money on her than I did on myself. I obsessed about getting her in the best dog obedience school. And, of course, dog toys, vet trips, grooming, and specialty food topping became part of my monthly budget.

Everything came full circle for me this past winter. I was at the pet store and saw dog slippers. I thought to myself, *Zoë needs those*, so I got her a set so her feet wouldn't be cold when we went on our walks. That evening I got out the new slippers and put them on her feet. As we started out of the house, I stepped on one of her squeaky toys (a rubber newspaper) and stuck it in my pocket so she would have something to play with. Then it dawned on me—I'm fetching *her* slippers and *her* newspaper!

Who exactly owns who here?

Sure we sometimes go overboard for our furry pals. And as you turn the pages of this book, you may come to recognize yourself (or someone you know). My guess is that as dog owners, we all have two things in common: we love our dogs and we don't actually own them—they own us.

Chaz Chapman
Co-creator of Barkford

...you have a bumper sticker that says My Dog Is an Honor Student at the Acme Dog Academy.

You Know Your Dog Owns You If...

...you use your frequent flier miles to upgrade your dog to first class.

...you won't eat chocolate because your dog can't eat chocolate.

... the studs on his collar are family heirlooms.

... her chew toys are made by Gucci.

You Know Your Dog Owns You If...

... you install an air conditioner in the doghouse, while your house has only a ceiling fan.

... you frequently trade recipes for homemade dog biscuits with other dog owners.

... you've had her portrait painted.

You Know Your

... you claim him as a dependent on your tax forms.

... people say you look like your dog and you think it's a compliment.

... you pretend to be blind so your dog can go into stores with you.

... you have a baby monitor beside his bed.

You Know Your Dog Owns You If...

...you know which of the 31 flavors of ice cream your dog likes best.

...you subscribe to the Bone of the Month Club.

...you talk baby talk to your dog no matter who is in the room.

... you own at least two T-shirts with your dog's picture on them in case one is dirty.

You Know Your Dog Owns You If...

… the dog groomer is on your speed dial.

… your ATM password is your dog's birthday.

… you frequently host doggy slumber parties.

You Know Your Dog Owns You If...

...you take her to obedience school and ask for college credits.

...you send birthday cards to your dog's day care provider.

...you're a major stockholder in a stain and odor removal company.

You Know Your

... he knows the difference between imported spring water and tap water.

Dog Owns You If...

… you find plastic sandwich bags in your pants pockets. And you hate sandwiches.

… you've built a Web site for him.

… you win a drawing for a professional photo session and use it for your dog.

… your Christmas cards are from both you and your dog.

… you let her eat dog biscuits in bed.

You Know Your Dog Owns You If…

… she has her own e-mail address.

… her name is on your return address labels.

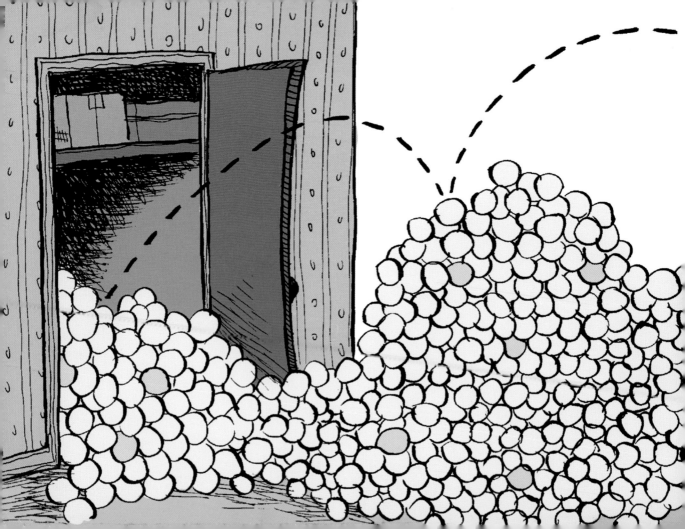

You Know Your Dog Owns You If...

...fetch is your favorite sport.

...you decide to buy clothes based on how likely
   it is that they will show dog hair ... and whether
   or not they will match her outfits.

...you bought an RV because it's easier than
   finding a hotel that would allow dogs.

... you chose your bank because the tellers give out doggy treats at the drive-thru window.

...you find yourself being overly quiet when your dog takes a nap.

You Know Your Dog Owns You If...

...you refer to him as Junior.

...you've attended the separation anxiety seminar at your doggy day care more than once.

...the only instrument you can play is a dog whistle.

...you quit your job to spend more time with your dog.

You Know Your

...whenever you need to make a difficult decision, you wonder *What would my dog do?*

Dog Owns You If...

… you've recently invested in a complete set of *Lassie* TV shows on DVD.

… you have ultrasound pictures of your dog.

… you've never let her see the end of *Old Yeller*.

… you hire Richard Simons as a personal trainer for your dog.

…you take a gourmet cooking class to spice up his meals.

You Know Your Dog Owns You If…

…pet health care insurance is an issue that concerns you.

…you have your recliner reupholstered in rawhide.

…2:00 A.M. walks have become a nightly ritual.

...you bought him a plush
toy so he won't get lonely.

... you include her in your nightly prayers.

You Know Your Dog Owns You If...

... your house is broken into during the night and you're glad your dog's sleep wasn't disturbed.

... you check her horoscope every day.

... you've secretly registered her to vote.

... you have her sweaters dry-cleaned.

You Know Your Dog Owns You If...

...you bought the expensive ergonomically correct dog crate.

...you've traced his genealogy.

...you worry that some TV shows might be too violent or explicit for your dog to watch.

... you feel guilty when you look at another dog.

You Know Your

... your shirts are monogrammed with AKC.

Dog Owns You If...

... she is executor of your will.

... you almost got into a fist fight when someone called your dog a mutt.

... your phone bill has charges on it for the Pet Psychic.

… you always leave the toilet seat up.

You Know Your Dog Owns You If...

...you've decided that you can't get married while your dog is alive.

...you've tasted his food to make sure it's fresh.

...you've recorded him barking on your answering machine.

You Know Your Dog Owns You If...

...you throw a ball, your dog lies down, and you chase after the ball.

...you throw a ball, your dog lifts her head, and you chase after the ball.

...you find leftovers in your refrigerator and can't remember if they are for you or your dog.

... more than once you've forgotten which toothbrush is yours and which is your dog's.

...he takes up more space on the bed than you do.

You Know Your Dog Owns You If...

...you think doggy drool is cute.

...you use a loofah to bathe him.

...his bed is made of cashmere.

...you spend hours comparing the labels of
   "organic" dog food.

Dog Owns You If...

...sometimes you let your dog walk you.

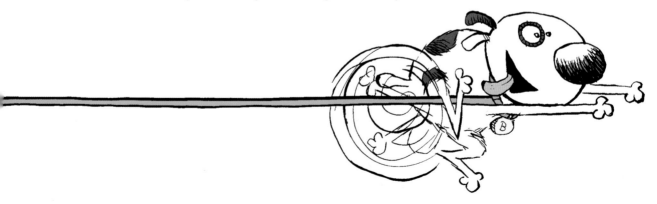

You Know Your Dog Owns You If...

… you don't have a garbage disposal because
   your dog likes to eat the table scraps.

… you sing "(How Much Is) That Doggie in the
   Window" to help your dog fall asleep.

… buffalo wings, chips, and soda means it's time
   to watch the Westminster Dog Show!

...no matter what gourmet dog food costs, it's never too much.

… you hate cats for no reason.

You Know Your Dog Owns You If...

... you've had a star named after her.

... you've lobbied the Olympic Committee to include the dog paddle among the swimming events.

... you haven't been out of the house alone in ten years.

You Know Your Dog Owns You If...

…you hired an interior designer to update your doghouse.

…you bring him his slippers.

…you have a tattoo of your dog in a private place.

… you had one of your car windows permanently removed.

You Know Your

... you overreact when the person at the DMV
tells you that someone else already has a
vanity license plate with your dog's name on it.

... you shop for furniture that will match your dog.

... you sign up for a couples massage class and
bring your dog.

... you bought this book for your dog.

... you plan your vacations around your dog's interests.

You Know Your Dog Owns You If...

... you always say grace before your dog eats.

... you let him win at tug-of-war to boost his self-esteem.

... you give him a piggyback ride when he is too tired to walk.

You Know Your Dog Owns You If...

...she has her own placemat on the table.

...her bandana is made of silk.

...you soak her chew toys in gravy.

...you know that she prefers squeaky toys that
play in the key of G major.

... your remote control doubles as a chew toy.

… you find dog biscuits in the strangest places.

…the only reason you have a webcam is so you can see your dog while you're at work.

You Know Your Dog Owns You If…

…you think his breath is actually kind of sweet.

…he is in your wedding photo.

You Know Your

... you own two treadmills; one for you and one for your dog.

Dog Owns You If...

… your dog is the benefactor of your life insurance policy.

… every window in your car has wet nose smears.

… you list your dog as the contact person in case of an emergency.

You Know Your Dog Owns You If...

... you wait until he goes into the other room
before you vacuum.

... he gets angry when you make noise during
dog food commercials.

... you help him stretch before you both go on
a run.

... you get his nails manicured by a professional.

... you celebrate his birthday seven times a year.

When they're not trying on funny hats, Chaz Chapman and Stacy Curtis try to be serious cartoonists. Together, they created "Barkford," a comic panel that appeared in *Dog Fancy* magazine from 2000-2003. Chaz writes and Stacy draws "Barkford."

Chaz Chapman is a husband, father, and pet owner who sometimes draws and writes cartoons. He is a member of the National Cartoonists Society and has been published in a variety of publications and on Web sites. Chaz lives in Portland, Oregon, with his wife, Catherine; daughter, Christina; and dog, Zoë.

Stacy Curtis is the award-winning editorial cartoonist for *The Times of Northwest Indiana*. His cartoons are distributed by Artizans. He has been cursed with a girl's name since birth.

Chaz Chapman (*left*), Stacy Curtis (*right*)